HOW DOES IT WORK?

A Book of Questions & Answers

By Jack Long

Illustrated by Vern McKissack

Cover by Stuart Trotter

GALLERY BOOKS
An Imprint of W. H. Smith Publishers Inc.
112 Madison Avenue
New York City 10016

Why does a wagon have to be pulled?

For a wagon—or anything—to move, a force is needed. When you pull or push a wagon, your energy is the force that makes the wheels roll over the ground. The harder you pull, or the more force you use, the faster it will go. If you don't pull the wagon, it will not move.

What makes my bicycle go?

The same force that makes your wagon go makes your bicycle go—and that's your energy. The pedals on your bike are connected to a small wheel with teeth called a *gear*. These teeth hold a loop of chain that runs between that gear and another gear on the back wheel. When you push the pedals the front gear turns. The chain moves and turns the back gear, which turns the back wheel of your bike, and you're off!

ENGINE

GAS TANK

What makes a car go?

You probably know about the engine, the part of a car that makes noise. It is also the part that makes the car go. A car is a very complicated machine. When the driver turns the key, the engine starts. Gasoline mixed with air feeds the engine and keeps it running. The engine makes the wheels turn and that makes the car go.

Why does a boat float?

A toy sailboat bobs along in your bathtub. An ocean liner plows through the waves. Both of these boats float—or stay on top of the water—because they weigh less than the water. That is, the weight of the boat and the space inside it is less than the weight of the water.

What is a submarine?

A submarine is a special kind of boat that can go either on top of or under the water. Submarines are built with lots of empty spaces inside them. When the submarine floats on top of the water, the spaces are filled with air. When the submarine dives underwater, special doors are opened and the air is replaced with sea water. The water is heavier than the air, so it makes the submarine sink under the water.

How does a space suit work?

Space suits cover and protect people in space. Since there is no air or water in space, they have to be carried in a special pack on the astronaut's back. The helmet, which covers the face and head, has a radio inside so the astronaut can speak to and hear other people. The suit itself has several special layers. One keeps out dust, and another keeps the temperature adjusted so the astronaut doesn't get too hot or too cold.

How does a refrigerator stay cold?

On a warm day, you reach into your refrigerator for cold juice or some nice cool yogurt. The refrigerator stays cold because it contains a liquid that *absorbs,* or soaks up, heat. Inside the refrigerator the liquid moves through pipes to the area where the food is kept. There it soaks up all the heat in the air. Since all the heat is now in the liquid, the air around the food is cool. The liquid travels to another area where a fan cools it off, and it's ready to start the job all over again!

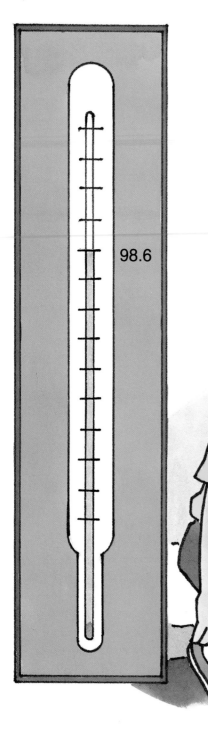

98.6

How does a thermometer tell my temperature?

A thermometer tells you how warm your body is. The small glass bulb at the bottom of the thermometer holds mercury, a silvery liquid that *expands,* or takes up more space, when it gets warm. The warmth of your mouth heats the mercury so it moves up the glass tube of the thermometer. The warmer you are, the higher up the tube the mercury goes. The tube is marked with lines and numbers, so you can see exactly what your temperature is. If you are not sick, your temperature is probably about 98.6 degrees.

How can a scale tell my weight?

When you step on the scale in the doctor's office your weight makes one end of a balance beam go down and the other end go up—just like a seesaw with only one person on it. Small weights on the balance beam are moved until the two ends of the beam are level. The numbers next to the weights tell how much you weigh. You can also tell your weight on a smaller scale like the one people often have in their bathrooms.

What is a magnet?

A magnet is a special piece of metal that can pull other metals to it with an invisible force. When you put two magnets near each other you can feel how strong this force is. A magnet has two ends, or poles, called north and south. The opposite poles of magnets attract each other. If you put the north end of one magnet near the south end of another magnet the two will pull together. If you put the two south ends or the two north ends together, the magnets push apart.

How does a compass work?

Could you find your way back from a strange place? If you knew whether to go north, south, east or west you could use a magnetic compass to help you. This kind of compass works because the earth has north and south poles that are powerful magnets. The small needle on a compass is a magnet, too. Since the opposite poles of any two magnets attract each other, the earth's north magnetic pole attracts the needle of the compass. The needle, often painted red, points to north. Now you can head home!

How can I see myself in a mirror?

You know that you can see through a glass window. Like windows, mirrors are made of highly polished glass. But instead of being clear, the back of a mirror is covered with a special silver coating that light cannot go through. When light hits the silver coating, it bounces back at you, and you see yourself reflected in the mirror. Wow, are you cute!

What is electricity?

Everything—air, water, even people—is made up of tiny, tiny parts called *atoms.* Atoms are so small you cannot see them. Atoms have even tinier parts called *electrons.* The electrons have a special power, or charge. Sometimes electrons use their special power to break free from their atoms and move around. Electricity is made when many electrons move in the same direction along a path. Electricity does so many things. It makes the lights go on, it makes your television work, and it even runs your tape recorder!

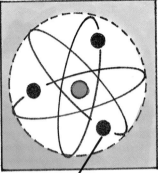

ATOM

ELECTRON

How does a light bulb work?

Inside a glass light bulb is a frame made of a glass tube, a glass rod, and wires. This framework supports a coil of wire called a *filament.* When you turn on a lamp, electricity enters at the bottom of the bulb and travels to the filament. The filament becomes so hot it glows, giving off the bright light you need to see.

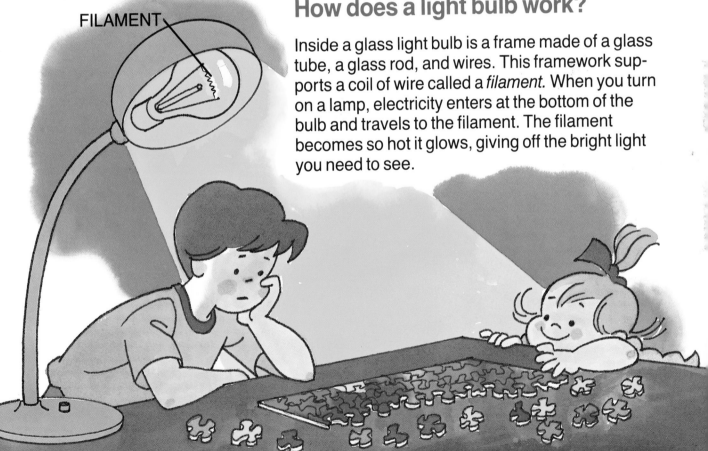

FILAMENT

What makes a doorbell ring?

The push button outside your door is connected by wires to the electrical system of your home. When the button is pressed by a visitor, it turns on the electricity. The electrical power makes the buzzer buzz or the bell ring.

How does a key lock a door?

A lock in a door has a metal bolt that slides back and forth when moved by a key. Along the edge of the key is a pattern of small notches. The key's notches fit into the lock like two pieces of a puzzle fit together. When the key is turned, it slides the bolt into a metal plate inside the door frame. Click! Now, the door is locked!

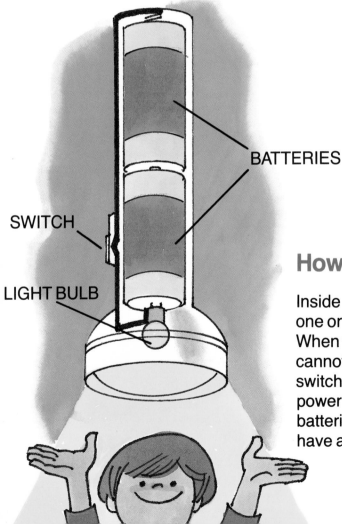

BATTERIES

SWITCH

LIGHT BULB

How does a flashlight work?

Inside the metal or plastic case of a flashlight are one or more batteries that store electrical power. When the flashlight is turned off, the electricity cannot get from the batteries to the bulb. When you switch on the flashlight, you make a path for the power to follow. Electrical power flows from the batteries, through the switch, to the bulb. You then have a small, bright light shining in the darkness!

How does a magnifying glass work?

A magnifying glass is a curved, clear piece of glass called a *lens.* If you hold it close to an object, the lens spreads out the light rays that pass through it. Your eyes see the spread out rays, which make the object appear larger than it really is.

How does a camera take a picture?

With photographs, you can always look at people and places
important to you—even if they are far away. The film in a camera
has a coating that reacts to light. When you snap a picture, you let
light inside the camera. It hits the film, and leaves an invisible picture
there. Then, when the film is developed by being placed in a special
liquid, the picture you took appears. It is then printed on paper and
you have a photograph!

How does a plane get into the air?

Planes use very strong engines to get up into the air. As the plane goes down the runway, it moves faster and faster. The pilot makes the back, or tail, lift slightly. Then, as the plane gains speed, the pilot raises the front, or nose, of the plane. The plane begins to climb as the wind rushes under it. You are in the air—have a nice flight!

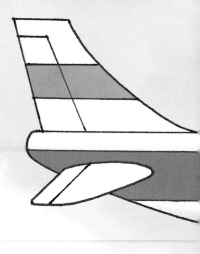

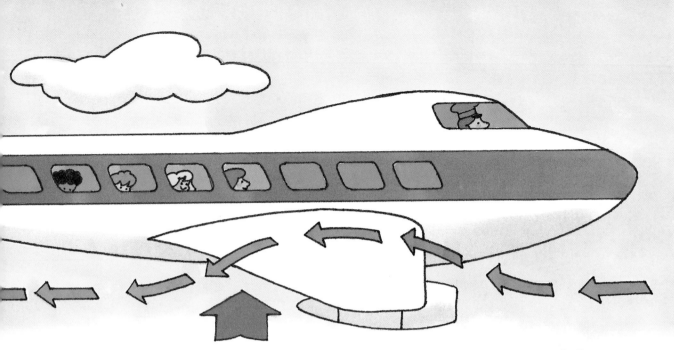

How does a plane stay up in the air?

An airplane's wings are curved on the top so that, when the plane is flying, the air going over the top of the wings moves faster than the air going under them. The air going under the wings is slower but stronger. It pushes up against the wings, lifting the plane and keeping it in the air. The plane is pushed forward through the air by its strong engines.

How does a piano make music?

There is more to a piano than the black and white keys you see. Inside there are more than 200 metal strings stretched from one end of the piano to the other. When you strike a key, it makes a small wooden hammer hit certain strings. That makes the strings move quickly back and forth, or *vibrate*. The vibrating strings make noise, which you hear as music.

Why does a clock tick?

Do you wake up in the morning to the sound of a ringing alarm clock? The power for one kind of clock comes from a metal coil called a *mainspring*. The mainspring's movement is controlled by a set of large and small gears (wheels with teeth). As the edges of two of the turning gears catch together, you hear *tick-tock-tick-tock*.

How does a radio work?

At a radio station music and voices are sent out into the air as invisible electrical signals. Your radio uses electric paths, or *circuits,* to pick up the signals out of the air and turn them back into words and music. It then plays them loud enough for you to hear.

How does television work?

Television is a combination of pictures and sound. The picture you see begins with a television camera. This special camera uses light and electricity to see and hear. It turns the picture and sound into a series of electrical signals. These signals are then sent by an antenna or cable to your television, which changes them back into what you see and hear. Most of the time, the picture and sounds are stored on tape, and then played back later for your television. That is why you can see the same show more than one time.

Why does a balloon float?

For a balloon to float in the air, it must weigh less than the air around it. Balloons that float are often filled with *helium*. Helium weighs less than the air around us, so the balloons float. If you blow up a balloon yourself, it will not float because your breath is the same weight as the air.

What makes my kite fly?

A kite is a very light plastic or wooden frame covered with paper, plastic or cloth. A long string is attached to one end. If you stand with your back to the wind and hold up the kite, the wind will pick it up and carry it into the sky. The force of the wind keeps the kite going higher and higher in the air. Hold on tight to the string or the kite will blow away!

How does a telephone work?

A telephone has two main parts. The part you speak into is called the *transmitter.* The part you listen to is called the *receiver.* When you talk into the transmitter, it turns your words into electrical signals. It then sends them over wires to another phone. That phone uses its receiver to change the signals back into words again. Since all telephones have both a receiver and a transmitter, you can talk to anyone on any other telephone!

How does a vacuum cleaner work?

An electric motor inside a vacuum cleaner turns a fan. The fan pushes air out of the vacuum cleaner. Air from the room rushes in to take its place. The air that rushes in carries dust, dirt, and small objects. They are stored in a disposable paper bag that fits inside the vacuum cleaner.

Why does popcorn pop?

Popcorn is made from dried kernels of corn. When you heat the corn, tiny drops of water inside the kernels turn into steam. The steam wants to escape, but it can't. The only way for it to get out is to break open the kernel. When the kernel pops you have popcorn!

Why does soda fizz?

Whether you call it soda, pop, or tonic, soda pop is a mixture of water, sugar, salt, flavorings, and a special kind of air called *carbon dioxide.* The fizz you see is tiny bubbles of carbon dioxide. When a bottle or can of soda is opened, all the bubbles rush to the top. You see all the bubbles as fizz. Sometimes those tricky little bubbles can even pop up and tickle your nose!

How is a record made?

By now, you know that sounds can be turned into electrical signals. To make a record, music and voices are turned into electrical signals. Then, those signals are fed into a machine that turns them into a series of wavy grooves that are imprinted on a plastic disc. Many, many copies are made of that disc. We call one of those copies a record.

How does my record player work?

The needle on the tone arm of your record player reads all the grooves on a record, and turns them back into electrical signals. The record player turns those electrical signals into sounds and words again, and makes them loud enough for you to hear.

How does a tape recorder work?

Tape recorders have two wheels, or reels, of tape, which store electrical signals. In a cassette recorder, both of those reels are inside the plastic case. The tape recorder does two things. It makes the tape move from one wheel to another. It also changes words into electrical signals and changes those signals back into words. When you *record* a voice or music, the machine puts signals onto the tape. When you *play* a tape, the recorder reads the signals and changes them back into words and sounds for you to hear.

MEOW